creepy creatures

CONTENTS

Published by Creative Paperbacks
P.O. Box 227, Mankato, Minnesota 56002
Creative Paperbacks is an imprint of
The Creative Company
www.thecreativecompany.us

Design and production by Ellen Huber
Art direction by Rita Marshall
Printed in the United States of America

Photographs by 123rf (Adrian Hillman), Bigstock
(Kurt Holter), Biosphoto (Guy Piton), Dreamstime
(Cammeraydave, Pablo Caridad, Fred De Bailliencourt,
ginasanders, Isselee), Getty Images (Tim Ridley),
iStockphoto (Ammit, Evgeniy Ayupov, David Gomez,
Eric Isselée, TommyIX), Science Photo Library
(Dr. Jeremy Burgess), Shutterstock (ajt, Bogomaz,
Kris Chambers, Melinda Fawver, Petr Jilek, Paleka,
PRILL Mediendesign und Fotografie), SuperStock
(Animals Animals, GAP, Minden Pictures), Veer
(lantapix, peapop, titelio)

Library of Congress Cataloging-in-Publication Data
Bodden, Valerie.
Slugs / by Valerie Bodden.
p. cm. — (Creepy creatures)
Summary: A basic introduction to slugs, examining
where they live, how they grow, what they eat, and
the unique physical traits that help to define them,
such as their slimy bodies and tentacles.
Includes bibliographical references and index.
ISBN 978-1-60818-233-6 (hardcover)
ISBN 978-0-89812-796-6 (pbk)
1. Slugs (Mollusks)—Juvenile literature. I. Title.
QL430.4.B63 2013
594'.3—dc23   2011050283

9 8 7 6 5 4 3 2

slugs

VALERIE BODDEN

CREATIVE
PAPER BACKS

It is a cloudy spring day.

You are playing in the park.

You pick up a rock. You

see something gray and

slimy crawling in the mud.

It is a slug!

Slugs are **mollusks**. They have no bones or legs. The bottom of a slug's body is made up of a strong **muscle** called the foot. Slugs have four **tentacles** (*TEN-tuh-kulz*) on their head. Two tentacles have eyes on the ends. The other two are for smelling and tasting.

Slugs have soft and slimy bodies that are good for gripping plants

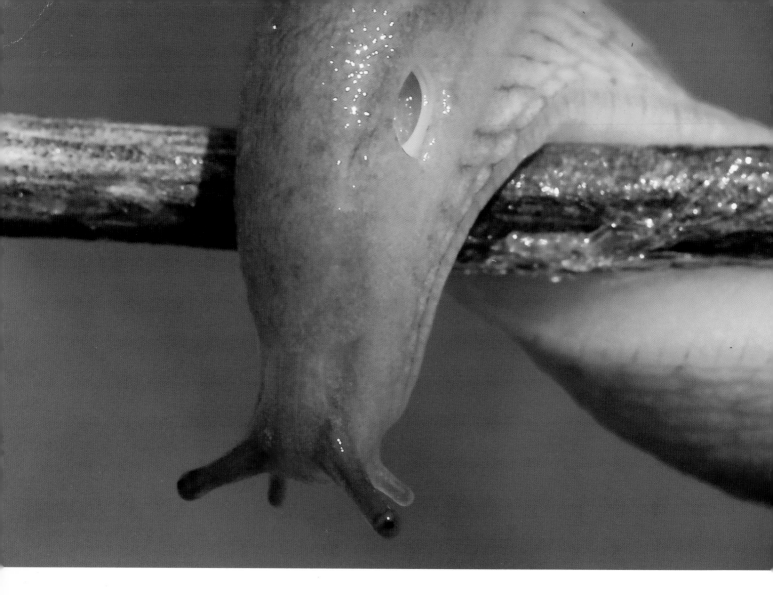

Most slugs are gray, tan, or yellow.

Slugs can be smaller than your fingernail.

Some slugs are orange or red in color

Or they can be bigger

than a grown-up's hand!

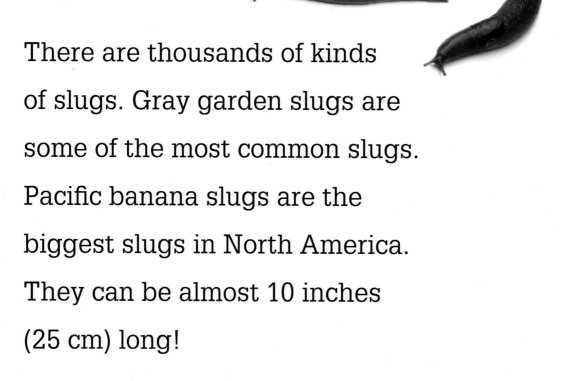

There are thousands of kinds
of slugs. Gray garden slugs are
some of the most common slugs.
Pacific banana slugs are the
biggest slugs in North America.
They can be almost 10 inches
(25 cm) long!

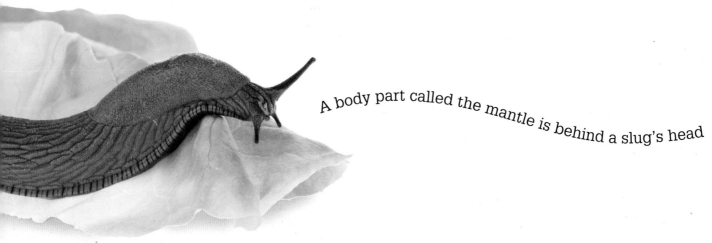

A body part called the mantle is behind a slug's head

Many banana slugs are yellow (as shown here), but others are spotted and brown

Leopard slugs like to live in places close to people

Slugs live in wet places such as forests, grasslands, and gardens. Many slugs make their homes underground. Slugs have to watch out for **predators**. Birds, snakes, and frogs eat slugs. So do turtles and rats.

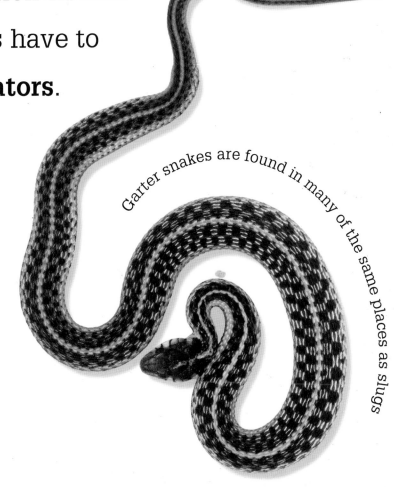

Garter snakes are found in many of the same places as slugs

All slugs are both male and female. This means that all slugs can lay eggs. Most slugs lay 20 to 30 eggs at a time. But some lay up to 100 eggs! Young slugs quickly grow into adults. Some slugs live only a few months. Others can live more than two years.

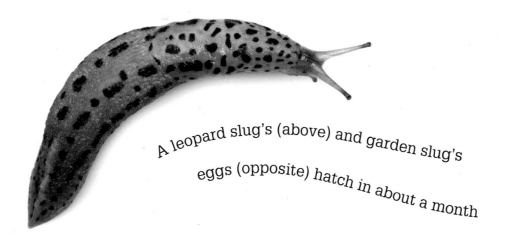

A leopard slug's (above) and garden slug's eggs (opposite) hatch in about a month

Red slugs live in gardens and climb up plants to reach food

Most slugs eat plants. They use their rough tongues to scrape at leaves. Some slugs eat snails and worms.

A slug's foot is covered with mucus (*MEW-kus*), or slime. The mucus helps the slug slide slowly across the ground. A slug leaves a trail of slime

Slug mucus is so sticky that it feels like glue when it dries

behind it. Some slugs can even hang from strings of mucus! Slug mucus tastes bad to predators.

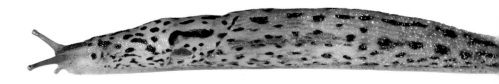

Slugs eat many plants but stay away from those with fuzzy leaves

Some kinds of slugs kill plants in people's gardens. But some people keep other kinds of slugs as pets. It can be fun finding and watching these slimy creepy creatures!

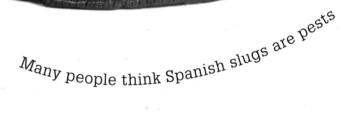

Many people think Spanish slugs are pests

MAKE A SLUG

Make a slug out of a clear plastic cup. First, tape a piece of colored paper to the inside walls of the cup. Lay the cup on its side. The bottom of the cup is your slug's head. Draw a mouth on it. Have a grown-up cut two small slits into the cup, right above the head. Stick the handle of a plastic spoon into each slit. Now you have tentacles with eyes on top!

GLOSSARY

mollusks: animals with soft bodies that are often covered by a shell

muscle: a part of the body that helps an animal move

predators: animals that kill and eat other animals

tentacles: long, thin, bendable growths on an animal that can be used for grabbing or feeling things or for moving

READ MORE

Henwood, Chris, and Barrie Watts. *Snails and Slugs*. Mankato, Minn.: Sea-to-Sea Publications, 2005.

Jennings, Terry J. *Bugs and Slugs*. Laguna Hills, Calif.: QEB Publishing, 2005.

WEB SITES

BioKIDS: Snails and Slugs
http://www.biokids.umich.edu/critters/Gastropoda/pictures/
Find pictures of different kinds of slugs and snails.

Enchanted Learning: Slugs
http://www.enchantedlearning.com/subjects/invertebrates/mollusk/gastropod/Slugprintout.shtml
Learn more about slugs, and print out a picture of a slug to color.

INDEX